BOSTON TERRIERS

KATIE LAJINESS

Big Buddy Books
An Imprint of Abdo Publishing
abdopublishing.com

BIG BUDDY DOGS

abdopublishing.com

Published by Abdo Publishing, a division of ABDO, PO Box 398166, Minneapolis, Minnesota 55439.
Copyright © 2018 by Abdo Consulting Group, Inc. International copyrights reserved in all countries.
No part of this book may be reproduced in any form without written permission from the publisher.
Big Buddy Books™ is a trademark and logo of Abdo Publishing.

Printed in the United States of America, North Mankato, Minnesota.
092017
012018

THIS BOOK CONTAINS
RECYCLED MATERIALS

Cover Photo: Getty Images.
Interior Photos: Elsa/Getty Images (p. 11); Getty Images (pp. 5, 7, 13, 15, 17, 19, 21, 23, 25, 27, 29, 30); SOTK2011/Alamy Stock Photo (p. 9).

Coordinating Series Editor: Tamara L. Britton
Contributing Editor: Jill Roesler
Graphic Design: Jenny Christensen

Publisher's Cataloging-in-Publication Data

Names: Lajiness, Katie, author.
Title: Boston terriers / by Katie Lajiness.
Description: Minneapolis, Minnesota : Abdo Publishing, 2018. | Series: Big buddy dogs |
    Includes online resources and index.
Identifiers: LCCN 2017943925 | ISBN 9781532112041 (lib.bdg.) | ISBN 9781614799115 (ebook)
Subjects: LCSH: Boston terrier--Juvenile literature. | Dogs--Juvenile literature.
Classification: DDC 636.72--dc23
LC record available at https://lccn.loc.gov/2017943925

CONTENTS

A POPULAR BREED

Around the world, there are more than 400 dog **breeds**. One of these is the Boston terrier. The Boston terrier's **ancestors** were bred from fighting dogs. But today, this breed is a gentle companion. Let's learn why Bostons are the twenty-first most popular breed in the United States!

This breed has yet to win Best in Show at the Westminster Kennel Club Dog Show.

THE DOG FAMILY

Dogs come in all shapes and sizes. Yet all dogs belong to the **Canidae** family. The name comes from the Latin word for dog, which is *canis*. This family includes coyotes, foxes, wolves, and more.

Humans and dogs have lived together for at least 16,000 years. In the beginning, humans **bred** them to hunt. Soon, they trained dogs to do other jobs such as guarding property and herding livestock.

Thousands of years ago, all dogs had jobs. Most people did not keep companion animals until the late 1700s.

BOSTON TERRIERS

The Boston terrier is truly an all-American **breed**. Around 1870, the breed began by crossing a bulldog with an English terrier. Some people called these dogs round heads or bull terriers.

The breed got the name Boston terrier in honor of the city from where it came. In 1891, the breed's supporters started the Boston Terrier Club of America.

The Boston terrier (*left*) looks different than the French bulldog (*right*). Boston terriers have pointed ears. French bulldogs have rounded ears.

Over time, the Boston terrier gained popularity. And in 1893, the **breed** joined the **American Kennel Club (AKC)**. It even became the preferred breed of two US presidents. And in 1979, the Boston terrier became the state dog of Massachusetts!

Did you know?

The AKC includes the Boston terrier in the Non-Sporting Group. Non-Sporting dogs include different breeds, sizes, and coats.

In 1922, Boston University made Rhett the Boston terrier its mascot.

WHAT THEY'RE LIKE

Boston terriers are very lively and athletic dogs. You will find them in agility trials, the obedience ring, and even tracking events.

A gentle **breed**, Bostons are easy to train. And, they are quiet dogs that rarely bark.

The breed's good mood and black-and-white coat earned it the nickname the American Gentleman.

COAT AND COLOR

These dogs have a short, smooth coat. They generally come in one of three colors. Boston terriers are either **brindle**, black, or **seal**. All Bostons have white on the **muzzle** and chest.

Did you know?

A circle of dark hair in the middle of a Boston terrier's head is called a Haggerty dot.

14

The Boston terrier was the first Non-Sporting dog breed started in the United States.

SIZE

Bostons are small dogs that weigh 15 to 25 pounds (7 to 11 kg). Males stand 15 to 17 inches (38 to 43 cm) tall. The females are somewhat smaller.

Their heads are square shaped with a short, wide **muzzle**. The **breed** also has large, wide-set eyes.

Boston terriers have a naturally short tail called a bobbed tail.

FEEDING

All dogs need food and water to supply energy. Quality dog food provides important **nutrients**. Dogs can eat moist, semimoist, and dry foods. Puppies eat three or more small meals a day. Adult dogs eat one to two times a day.

Dogs should eat the same amount of food every day. This way, they won't eat too much and become overweight.

CARE

Dogs require a lot of care. Boston terriers need regular brushing to keep their coats healthy. Sometimes, they need baths to stay clean. A dog should have its nails trimmed once a month. It should also have its teeth checked to avoid **infection**.

Did you know?

The shape of a Boston's head can cause its teeth to crowd. So, owners need to brush the dog's teeth regularly to keep them healthy.

Boston terriers do not like very hot or cold weather. These dogs prefer to live indoors with a consistent temperature.

All dogs need to visit a veterinarian. The vet can provide **vaccines** and health exams for a Boston terrier. He or she can also **spay** or **neuter** the dog.

During their first few months, puppies will need to see the vet several times. Adult dogs should visit the vet once a year for a checkup.

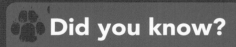

Did you know?

Snub-nosed dog breeds should not fly in airplanes. They have trouble breathing so high in the air.

During an exam, a vet will check your dog's ears for signs of infection.

Every dog needs a collar with identification tags. A **microchip** can also keep a dog safe. This way, an owner can find the pet if it gets lost.

At home, a crate offers a Boston terrier a place to rest. It can also help with housebreaking puppies.

Daily walks are important.
Most Bostons need at least
a half-hour walk every day.

PUPPIES

A Boston terrier mother is **pregnant** for about 63 days. Then, she gives birth to a **litter** of three to four puppies.

All puppies are born blind and deaf. After two weeks, they can see and hear. At three weeks, the puppies begin taking their first steps.

Puppies sleep 15 to 20 hours a day. At first, someone needs to show them the safest place to nap.

THINGS THEY NEED

At eight to 12 weeks old, Boston terrier puppies are ready for **adoption**. When the puppy comes home, its owner should begin obedience training as soon as it is settled.

Boston terrier puppies like to be active. So, they need daily exercise and training. A Boston terrier will be a loving companion for 12 to 14 years.

Basic obedience training includes learning to sit and stay.

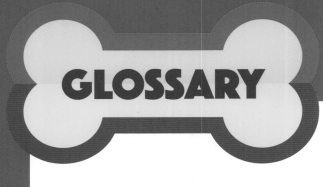

GLOSSARY

adoption the process of taking responsibility for a pet.

ancestor a family member from an earlier time.

American Kennel Club (AKC) an organization that studies and promotes interest in purebred dogs.

breed a group of animals sharing the same appearance and features. To breed is to produce animals by mating.

brindle having dark streaks or spots on a gray or brownish background.

Canidae (KAN-uh-dee) the scientific Latin name for the dog family. Members of this family are called canids. They include wolves, jackals, foxes, coyotes, and domestic dogs.

infection (ihn-FEHK-shuhn) the causing of an unhealthy condition by something harmful, such as bacteria.

litter all of the puppies born at one time to a mother dog.

microchip an electronic circuit placed under an animal's skin. A microchip contains identifying information that can be read by a scanner.

muzzle an animal's nose and jaws.

neuter (NOO-tuhr) to remove a male animal's reproductive glands.

nutrient (NOO-tree-uhnt) something found in food that living beings take in to live and grow.

pregnant having one or more babies growing within the body.

seal black with a reddish tone that can be seen in bright sunlight.

spay to remove a female animal's reproductive organs.

vaccine (vak-SEEN) a shot given to prevent illness or disease.

ONLINE RESOURCES

Booklinks
NONFICTION NETWORK
FREE! ONLINE NONFICTION RESOURCES

To learn more about Boston terriers, visit **abdobooklinks.com**. These links are routinely monitored and updated to provide the most current information available.

INDEX